# NUTRITION TIPS FOR TEEN ATHLETES

The Ultimate Handbook to Unlocking your Potential in Sports

**Juni Lund**

# TABLE OF CONTENTS

# INTRODUCTION

During adolescence, the body goes through significant physical and hormonal changes, making it a crucial period for growth and development. For teen athletes, these changes come with unique nutritional needs to support their athletic endeavors and overall well-being. Understanding these needs is essential in ensuring they perform optimally and maintain good health.

## *Here are some important factors to think about:*

### 1. Increased Energy Requirements:

Teen athletes have higher energy demands compared to sedentary individuals of the same age group. Their active lifestyles and participation in sports or physical activities result in increased calorie expenditure. Proper nutrition is vital to meet these energy needs and prevent deficits that could lead to fatigue, decreased performance, or potential health issues.

## 2. Essential Nutrients for Growth:

Adolescence is a critical time for growth and development, and adequate intake of essential nutrients is crucial. Protein, for instance, is essential for muscle growth and repair. Calcium and vitamin D are crucial for bone health, as peak bone mass is achieved during teenage years. Iron is important for red blood cell production and oxygen transport especially for teen female athletes during menstruation.

## 3. Balanced Macronutrient Intake:

A balanced diet that includes appropriate amounts of macronutrients (carbohydrates, proteins, and fats) is necessary to fuel teen athletes' activities effectively. Carbohydrates serve as the primary energy source for muscles, and adequate intake is essential for optimal performance. Protein aids in muscle repair and synthesis, while healthy fats support hormone production and overall health.

## 4. Hydration:

Proper hydration is fundamental for athletic performance and overall health. Teen athletes need to drink enough fluids before, during, and after exercise to replace the fluids lost through sweat. Dehydration can impair performance, lead to fatigue, and increase the risk of heat-related illnesses.

## 5. Timing of Meals and Snacks:

Teen athletes should pay attention to the timing of their meals and snacks to optimize energy levels during training and competitions. Eating a balanced meal 2-4 hours before exercise provides sufficient fuel, while a pre-exercise snack 30 minutes to an hour before can provide an additional energy boost. After exercise, they should consume a post-workout meal or snack to support muscle recovery and replenish energy stores.

## 6. Adequate Rest and Recovery:

Teen athletes often have busy schedules with school, training, and social commitments. It's essential to emphasize the importance of adequate rest and recovery to prevent burnout and reduce the risk of injuries. Sleep is a crucial component of recovery, as it allows the body to repair and rejuvenate.

## 7. Mindful Eating:

Promoting a positive relationship with food is vital for teen athletes. Encouraging them to focus on mindful eating and listen to their bodies' hunger and fullness cues helps establish healthy eating habits. Avoiding restrictive diets and embracing a balanced approach to nutrition can contribute to better overall well-being.

Understanding the unique needs of teen athletes is key to supporting their growth, performance, and overall health. Providing them with the right nutrition, hydration, and recovery strategies will empower them to thrive both on and off the field during this critical phase of their lives.

# SECTION ONE

# THE CONNECTION BETWEEN NUTRITION AND ATHLETIC PERFORMANCE

Proper nutrition plays a fundamental role in an athlete's performance, regardless of age or level of competition. The relationship between nutrition and athletic performance is complex and multifaceted, with nutrition directly influencing an athlete's energy levels, endurance, strength, and overall well-being. Here are some key aspects that highlight the connection between nutrition and athletic performance:

- **Energy Levels and Fueling:** Nutrition provides the body with the necessary fuel to perform at its best. Carbohydrates are the primary source of energy for athletes, as they are broken down into glucose and stored as glycogen in muscles. Adequate carbohydrate intake ensures that athletes have sufficient energy to sustain prolonged physical activities, enhancing endurance and preventing early fatigue.

- **Muscle Function and Recovery:** Protein intake is crucial for athletes to support muscle function, repair, and recovery. During intense exercise, muscle fibers undergo microtears, and consuming enough protein helps rebuild and strengthen these tissues. Amino acids, the building blocks of proteins, play a vital role in muscle repair and synthesis.

- **Hydration and Electrolyte Balance:** Proper hydration is essential for athletes to maintain optimal performance. Dehydration can lead to reduced blood volume, which negatively impacts circulation and nutrient delivery to muscles. It also impairs thermoregulation, increasing the risk of heat-related illnesses. Maintaining electrolyte balance is equally important, as electrolytes are critical for nerve and muscle function.

- **Nutrient Timing:** Timing of meals and snacks is crucial for athletes to optimize energy availability during exercise and support post-exercise recovery. Consuming a balanced meal a few hours before exercise provides sustained energy, while having a carbohydrate-rich snack shortly before can boost performance. After exercise, consuming a combination of carbohydrates and protein enhances glycogen replenishment and muscle recovery.

- **Immune Function:** Regular intense exercise can temporarily suppress the immune system, making athletes more susceptible to infections. Proper nutrition, including adequate vitamins and minerals, can help support immune function and reduce the risk of illness.

- **Mental Focus and Cognitive Performance:** Nutrition not only impacts physical performance but also mental focus and cognitive function. Properly fueled athletes are more alert and able to make better decisions during competition, leading to improved overall performance.

- **Injury Prevention and Recovery:** A well-balanced diet with sufficient nutrients can aid in injury prevention and recovery. Nutrients like vitamin C and zinc are essential for collagen synthesis, which plays a crucial role in maintaining healthy connective tissues.

The connection between nutrition and athletic performance is undeniable. Providing athletes with the right balance of macronutrients, micronutrients, and hydration ensures they have the energy, strength, and mental focus needed to excel in their sport. Proper nutrition not only enhances athletic performance but also contributes to overall health and well-being, helping athletes reach their full potential on and off the field.

# *Incorporating Nutrient-Dense Foods into the Diet*

"Eating the rainbow" refers to the practice of consuming a diverse array of colorful fruits and vegetables, each offering a unique combination of vitamins, minerals, and antioxidants. This concept emphasizes the importance of incorporating nutrient-dense foods into the diet of teen athletes. By including a wide variety of colorful produce, they can ensure they receive a broad spectrum of essential nutrients necessary for optimal athletic performance and overall health.

## Micronutrients for Health and Performance:

Fruits and vegetables are rich sources of various micronutrients that play vital roles in the body. For example:

- **Iron:** Found in leafy greens, beans, and fortified cereals, iron is crucial for oxygen transport in the blood, which is especially important during exercise when oxygen demands are higher.

- **Calcium:** Dairy products, leafy greens, and fortified plant-based milk are excellent sources of calcium, essential for maintaining strong bones and preventing stress fractures.

11

- **Vitamin C:** Citrus fruits, strawberries, bell peppers, and broccoli provide vitamin C, an antioxidant that supports the immune system and aids in tissue repair.

## Antioxidants for Recovery and Immune Support:

The vibrant colors in fruits and vegetables are often attributed to natural plant compounds called antioxidants. These antioxidants play a significant role in reducing oxidative stress in the body, which can result from intense exercise. By neutralizing free radicals, antioxidants aid in recovery, reduce muscle soreness, and support a healthy immune system.

## Fiber for Digestive Health and Satiety:

Fruits and vegetables are excellent sources of dietary fiber, which promotes healthy digestion and helps regulate blood sugar levels. Fiber also contributes to a feeling of fullness, helping athletes maintain a healthy body weight and avoid overeating.

## Phytochemicals for Performance and Disease Prevention:

Beyond essential vitamins and minerals, fruits and vegetables contain phytochemicals—naturally occurring compounds with potential health benefits. For example:

- **Beta-Carotene:** Found in orange and yellow fruits and vegetables like carrots and sweet potatoes, beta-carotene is converted into vitamin A in the body, supporting vision and skin health.

- **Lycopene:** Present in red fruits like tomatoes, lycopene is associated with cardiovascular health and may reduce the risk of certain cancers.

Incorporating a diverse range of fruits and vegetables into their diet can be a fun and creative process for teen athletes. Encouraging them to try new and colorful produce regularly will not only enhance their nutrient intake but also contribute to their overall enjoyment of food.

**Practical tips for incorporating nutrient-dense foods include:**

- Including a variety of fruits and vegetables in each meal, whether it's a colorful salad, a smoothie with mixed berries, or roasted vegetables as a side dish.

- Experimenting with different cooking methods to find ones that suit their taste preferences, such as steaming, grilling, or enjoying some fruits and vegetables raw.

- Trying seasonal produce and visiting local farmers' markets to discover fresh, locally grown options.

By making "eating the rainbow" a part of their daily routine, teen athletes can ensure they receive a well-rounded and nutrient-rich diet that supports their athletic endeavors and promotes overall health.

# SECTION TWO

# PRE-GAME PREPARATIONS

Proper pre-game preparations are essential for teen athletes to ensure they have the energy and focus needed to perform at their best. It involves strategic meal planning, snack choices, and considerations for timing to optimize performance and avoid discomfort during physical activity.

- **Timing is Key:** Proper Meal Planning Before Competitions. Timing meals appropriately before a competition is vital to ensure that athletes have enough energy to perform optimally without experiencing digestive issues or discomfort. This section will cover the following aspects:

- **The Pre-Competition Meal:** This meal should consist of easily digestible carbohydrates, moderate protein, and low-fat content to provide sustained energy and prevent gastrointestinal distress during exercise.

- **Carbohydrate Loading:** For events lasting longer than 90 minutes, such as long-distance running or swimming, Athletes can increase their carbohydrate intake in the days leading up to the event to maximize glycogen stores in muscles and liver, enhancing endurance.

- **Hydration:** Hydration is equally important before the competition. The significance of starting the event well-hydrated and provide tips on proper hydration in the hours leading up to the start time.

- **Snack Smart:** Energizing with Healthy Pre-Game Treats

For events that don't allow enough time for a full meal or during busy competition schedules, snacking can be an effective way to maintain energy levels. This section will cover the following:

- **Choosing the Right Snacks:** Healthy pre-game snack options that are rich in easily digestible carbohydrates, such as granola bars, bananas, or whole-grain crackers. These snacks can provide quick energy without causing bloating or discomfort during activity.

- **Portion Control:** It's essential for athletes to be mindful of portion sizes to avoid feeling too full or experiencing energy crashes during the event.

- **Supplements for Teens:** Debunking Myths and Ensuring Safe Use

Supplements shouldn't be used as a replacement for a healthy, balanced diet. However, some teen athletes may consider using supplements to enhance their performance.

# During the Game

During the game, teen athletes must maintain their energy levels, hydration, and focus to perform at their best. This section focuses on strategies to fuel the body and stay hydrated during competition, ensuring sustained performance and preventing fatigue.

- **Fueling Mid-Game:** Snacks and Hydration on the Field

- **Importance of On-the-Go Snacks:** Teen athletes may need a quick energy boost during the game, especially during extended or intense competitions.

- **Monitoring Energy Levels:** Teen athletes will learn to pay attention to their bodies' energy levels and hunger cues, helping them determine when and what type of snack they may need to maintain optimal performance.

# Strategies for Staying Energized during Extended Competitions

For events lasting longer than an hour, teen athletes need a game plan to keep their energy levels high throughout the competition. This section will cover the following:

- **Regular Hydration:** Emphasizing the importance of continuous hydration during extended competitions. Athletes should take advantage of breaks or timeouts to hydrate properly and avoid waiting until they feel thirsty.

- **Carbohydrate Intake:** Snacks like energy bars, fruit, or sandwiches can be helpful for refueling during breaks.

- **Electrolyte Replacement:** Prolonged physical activity can lead to electrolyte loss through sweat. It is very importance replacing electrolytes with sports drinks or electrolyte tablets to maintain proper fluid balance and prevent muscle cramps.

By incorporating smart fueling and hydration strategies during the game, teen athletes can sustain their energy levels focus, and endurance, allowing them to maintain peak performance from start to finish. These practices will contribute to improved athletic outcomes and reduced risk of fatigue-related errors or injuries during competition.

## *Post-Game Recovery*

Post-game recovery is a crucial phase for teen athletes, as it lays the foundation for their future performance and overall well-being. This section focuses on strategies to promote efficient recovery, repair muscles, and replenish energy stores after intense physical activity.

## The Importance of Post-Game Nutrition: Replenishing and Repairing

- **Nutrient Timing:** The importance of consuming a balanced meal or snack within the first hour after the game. This window of opportunity is known as the "glycogen replenishment window," where the body is most receptive to refueling glycogen stores in muscles.

- **Macronutrient Ratios:** Discussing the ideal macronutrient ratios for post-game nutrition, with an emphasis on carbohydrates to restore glycogen, proteins to support muscle repair and growth, and a moderate amount of healthy fats to aid nutrient absorption.

- **Combining Whole Foods and Supplements:** While whole foods should be the primary focus, the role of supplements like protein shakes or recovery drinks for athletes who struggle to eat immediately after a game.

## Protein's Function in Muscle Growth and Recovery

- **Protein Requirements:** Understanding the protein needs of teen athletes after a game. How protein intake assists in repairing damaged muscle fibers and promoting muscle growth.

- **High-Quality Protein Sources:** The various sources of high-quality protein, such as lean meats, poultry, fish, dairy, eggs, legumes, and plant-based options like tofu and quinoa.

- **Snacking for Recovery:** Suggesting protein-rich snacks like Greek yogurt with fruits, a turkey sandwich, or a protein smoothie to kickstart the recovery process.

Rehydration and Electrolyte Balance: Bouncing Back after Intense Exertion

- **Hydration after the Game:** The importance of rehydrating post-game to replenish fluid loss through sweat and restore proper hydration levels.

- **Electrolyte Replacement:** Discussing the significance of electrolyte replacement after exercise to maintain fluid balance and prevent muscle cramps.

- **Monitoring Hydration Status:** Encouraging teen athletes to monitor their urine color and pay attention to signs of dehydration, such as dark-colored urine or feeling thirsty.

Post-game recovery is an essential aspect of athletic training and performance. Proper nutrition and hydration during this phase ensure that teen athletes' bodies recover efficiently, reducing the risk of injuries, fatigue, and burnout. Implementing effective recovery strategies will enable them to bounce back quickly, feel energized, and be ready for the next training session or competition.

# SECTION THREE

# SPECIAL CONSIDERATIONS

In this section, we address specific considerations that may apply to certain teen athletes, focusing on managing weight, handling dietary restrictions, and addressing unique nutritional needs.

## *Addressing Weight Management Safely: Balancing Nutrition and Performance*

- **Promoting Healthy Practices:** Emphasizing the importance of adopting safe and healthy weight management practices, particularly for athletes involved in weight-class sports. Encourage teen athletes to prioritize their overall well-being and performance over rapid weight loss or extreme dieting.

- **Consulting Professionals:** Recommending that athletes seeking weight management guidance consult with sports dietitians, coaches, or healthcare professionals. These experts can help develop individualized plans that meet performance goals without compromising health.

- **Proper Nutrition for Weight Management:**
  Providing information on how to strike a balance
  between calorie intake and expenditure while
  ensuring adequate nutrient intake for optimal
  performance and recovery.

## *Handling Dietary Restrictions and Allergies: Navigating Challenges*

Understanding Dietary Restrictions: Some teen athletes may
have specific dietary restrictions due to religious, cultural, or
health reasons.

- **Managing Food Allergies:** Addressing the
  challenges faced by teen athletes with food allergies,
  such as gluten intolerance or nut allergies. Provide
  alternative food options to ensure they get the
  necessary nutrients while avoiding allergens.

- **Nutritional Supplementation:** Exploring the use
  of supplements for teen athletes with dietary
  restrictions or allergies, ensuring they obtain essential
  nutrients that may be lacking in their diets.

By addressing special considerations, teen athletes can
navigate challenges and find solutions to maintain a healthy
and balanced diet while catering to their individual needs.
Proper management of weight, dietary restrictions, and
allergies will allow them to focus on their sport, enhance

performance, and promote overall well-being. Encouraging open communication and collaboration with healthcare professionals is essential in ensuring their nutritional needs are met safely and effectively.

# CONCLUSION

**Achieving Long-Term Success: Making Nutrition a Lifestyle Choice**

- **Emphasizing Consistency:** Stressing the importance of consistent healthy eating habits rather than short-term restrictive diets. By adopting a balanced and sustainable approach to nutrition, teen athletes can better support their athletic goals and maintain good health in the long run.

- **Mindful Eating:** Encouraging teen athletes to be mindful of their food choices, hunger cues, and nutritional needs. Learning to listen to their bodies and make nourishing choices will help them develop a positive relationship with food and enhance overall well-being.

- **Building Healthy Habits:** Reinforcing the idea that proper nutrition is not just a one-time effort but an ongoing commitment. Cultivating healthy habits around eating, hydration, and recovery will contribute to improved athletic performance and overall quality of life.

**Emphasizing Health and Well-Being: A Holistic Approach to Athletic Performance**

**The Connection between Health and Performance:** Highlighting the direct relationship between good health and athletic success. Proper nutrition, hydration, and recovery contribute to enhanced physical and mental performance, reduced risk of injuries, and better overall outcomes in sports.

- **The Bigger Picture:** Encouraging teen athletes to view nutrition as one component of a holistic approach to their athletic journey. Emphasizing the importance of sleep, stress management, and a balanced lifestyle to support their physical and mental well-being.

By understanding their unique nutritional needs, making informed choices, and adopting sustainable habits, teen athletes can unlock their full potential, perform at their best, and lead a healthy and fulfilling life both on and off the field. It is a reminder that proper nutrition is not a short-term fix but a lifelong commitment to their well-being and athletic aspirations.

# SAMPLE MEAL PLANS FOR TEEN ATHLETES

**Breakfast:**

- ➤ Scrambled eggs with spinach and whole-grain toast
- ➤ Greek yogurt with mixed berries and honey
- ➤ Orange juice

**Lunch:**

- ➤ Grilled chicken breast with quinoa and steamed broccoli
- ➤ Mixed green salad with cherry tomatoes, cucumbers, and vinaigrette dressing
- ➤ Fresh fruit salad

**Dinner:**

- ➤ Baked salmon with sweet potato wedges
- ➤ Steamed asparagus with lemon zest
- ➤ Brown rice

**Breakfast:**

- ➤ Overnight oats with almond milk, chia seeds, and sliced bananas

- ➤ Almond butter on whole-grain toast

- ➤ Apple slices

**Lunch:**

- ➤ Turkey and avocado wrap with whole-grain tortilla

- ➤ Carrot sticks with hummus

- ➤ Low-fat yogurt with granola

**Dinner:**

- ➤ Stir-fried tofu with mixed vegetables and brown rice

- ➤ Edamame with a sprinkle of sea salt

- ➤ Pineapple slices

**Breakfast:**

- ➤ Whole-grain pancakes with fresh berries and maple syrup

- ➤ Cottage cheese with sliced peaches

## Lunch:

- ➤ Grilled shrimp with quinoa and sautéed spinach

- ➤ Cherry tomatoes with balsamic glaze

- ➤ Watermelon cubes

## Dinner:

- ➤ Baked chicken breast with roasted sweet potatoes

- ➤ Steamed green beans

- ➤ Mixed fruit salad

## Breakfast:

- ➤ Smoothie with spinach, banana, Greek yogurt, and almond milk

- ➤ Almond butter on whole-grain toast

- ➤ Orange slices

## Lunch:

- ➤ Veggie burger on a whole-grain bun with avocado and lettuce

- ➤ Baked sweet potato fries

- Cucumber slices with tzatziki sauce

**Dinner:**

- Grilled steak with quinoa and sautéed bell peppers
- Garden salad with balsamic vinaigrette
- Kiwi slices

# SNACK IDEAS FOR TEEN ATHLETES

- ❖ Trail mix with nuts, seeds, and dried fruit.

- ❖ Rice cakes topped with almond butter and banana slices

- ❖ Greek yogurt with honey and a sprinkle of granola.

- ❖ Carrot sticks with hummus or guacamole.

- ❖ Cottage cheese with pineapple chunks.

- ❖ Whole-grain crackers with cheese slices.

- ❖ Apple slices with peanut butter.

- ❖ Fresh berries and a handful of almonds.

- ❖ Energy bars made with oats, nuts, and dried fruits.

- ❖ Cherry tomatoes with mozzarella cheese and balsamic glaze.

- ❖ Frozen grapes for a refreshing treat.

- ❖ Homemade popcorn seasoned with nutritional yeast or a pinch of salt.

- ❖ Celery sticks with cream cheese or almond butter.

- ❖ Sliced cucumber with lemon juice and a dash of chili powder.

❖ Baby carrots with a side of Greek yogurt-based ranch dressing for dipping.

These sample meal plans and snack ideas provide a diverse range of nutritious options to fuel teen athletes for their training, competitions, and daily activities. It's essential to personalize these meal plans and snacks based on individual preferences, dietary needs, and specific athletic goals. Additionally, staying well-hydrated by drinking plenty of water throughout the day is crucial for maintaining optimal performance and overall health.

# PRE-GAME MEAL IDEAS

Pre-game meals are essential to provide teen athletes with the energy and nutrients they need to perform at their best during competitions or intense training sessions. The focus should be on easily digestible, nutrient-rich foods that fuel the body and support sustained energy. Here are some pre-game meal ideas for teen athletes:

- ✓ **Grilled Chicken with Sweet Potatoes and Green Beans:**

A balanced meal with lean protein from grilled chicken, complex carbohydrates from sweet potatoes, and fiber-rich green beans for sustained energy.

- ✓ **Whole-Grain Pasta with Tomato Sauce and Lean Turkey:**

Pasta provides easily digestible carbohydrates, and lean turkey offers protein for muscle support. Add a side of mixed vegetables for extra nutrients.

- ✓ **Quinoa Salad with Chickpeas and Mixed Vegetables:**

Quinoa is a complete protein source, and the chickpeas add additional protein and fiber. Mix in a variety of colorful vegetables for a nutrient-packed meal.

- ✓ **Brown Rice with Baked Salmon and Steamed Broccoli:**

Brown rice is a great source of complex carbohydrates, and salmon offers healthy fats and protein. Broccoli adds vitamins and minerals to the meal.

- ✓ **Turkey and Avocado Wrap:**

Fill a whole-grain wrap with sliced turkey, avocado, lettuce, and tomato for a balanced and portable pre-game meal.

- ✓ **Stir-Fried Tofu with Brown Rice and Vegetables:**

Tofu provides plant-based protein, and brown rice offers sustained energy. Stir-fry a mix of colorful vegetables for added nutrients and flavor.

- ✓ **Quinoa Bowl with Black Beans, Avocado, and Salsa:**

Quinoa is rich in protein and complex carbohydrates, and black beans add additional protein and fiber. Top with diced avocado and salsa for a flavorful meal.

- ✓ **Whole-Grain Sandwich with Lean Ham, Cheese, and Veggies:**

Use whole-grain bread, lean ham, and your favorite cheese for a balanced and convenient pre-game meal. Add lettuce, tomato, and cucumber slices for extra nutrition.

- ✓ **Grilled Shrimp with Jasmine Rice and Asparagus:**

Shrimp provides protein, while jasmine rice offers quick-digesting carbohydrates. Asparagus adds vitamins and minerals to the meal.

✓ **Vegetable Omelets with Whole-Grain Toast:** Whip up an omelet with eggs and your favorite vegetables for a protein-packed meal. Serve with whole-grain toast for additional carbohydrates.

Ensure you eat your pre-game meal at least 3-4 hours before the competition or training session to allow sufficient time for digestion. Customize these meal ideas based on your individual preferences, dietary needs, and the timing of your event. Stay well-hydrated by drinking water throughout the day to complement your pre-game meal and optimize your performance on the field or court.

# POST-GAME RECOVERY SNACKS

Post-game recovery snacks are crucial to replenish energy, support muscle repair, and aid in recovery after intense physical activity. Here are some nutritious and delicious post-game recovery snack options for teen athletes:

- **Chocolate Milk:**

A classic choice, chocolate milk provides a combination of carbohydrates and protein, making it an excellent option for replenishing glycogen stores and supporting muscle recovery.

- **Greek Yogurt with Berries:** Greek yogurt is high in protein and contains probiotics that aid digestion. Adding mixed berries provides antioxidants and natural sweetness.

- **Banana with Almond Butter:** Bananas are rich in carbohydrates and potassium, while almond butter offers healthy fats and protein, making this a satisfying and nutrient-packed snack.

- **Trail Mix:** Create your own trail mix with a mix of nuts, seeds, dried fruits, and a few dark chocolate chips for a tasty and energy-boosting combination.

- **Hummus and Whole-Grain Pita:** Hummus provides protein and healthy fats, and whole-grain pita offers complex carbohydrates to refuel energy stores.

- **Turkey Sandwich:** A turkey sandwich on whole-grain bread provides a balance of protein and carbohydrates, and you can add lettuce, tomato, and avocado for extra nutrients.

- **Cottage Cheese with Pineapple:** Cottage cheese is rich in protein, and pineapple offers natural sweetness and contains bromelain, an enzyme that may aid in reducing inflammation.

- **Apple Slices with Cheese:** Pair apple slices with your favorite cheese for a combination of carbohydrates, protein, and calcium.

- **Energy Bars:** Choose energy bars with whole food ingredients, like nuts, seeds, dried fruits, and oats, for a convenient and nutrient-dense post-game snack.

- **Rice Cakes with Nut Butter and Sliced Banana:** Rice cakes offer easily digestible carbohydrates, while nut butter and banana provide protein and potassium.

Remember to consume your post-game recovery snack within 30 minutes to an hour after exercise to take advantage of the glycogen replenishment window and support muscle recovery. Hydration is also crucial, so make sure to drink water or a sports drink to rehydrate after intense physical activity. Enjoy these snacks as part of a balanced post-game meal or incorporate them into your recovery routine to help you perform at your best in the next game or training session.

Made in United States
Orlando, FL
07 June 2024

47592624R00024